Williams 1969 - 1998
Photo Album
30 Years of Grand Prix Racing

By Peter Nygaard

Iconografix
Photo Album Series

Iconografix
PO Box 446
Hudson, Wisconsin 54016 USA

Library of Congress Card Number: 98-75270

ISBN 1-58388-000-3

99 00 01 02 03 04 05 5 4 3 2 1

Printed in the United States of America

Cover and book design by Shawn Glidden
Edited by Dylan Frautschi

Iconografix Inc. exists to preserve history through the publication of notable photographic archives and the list of titles under the Iconografix imprint is constantly growing. Transportation enthusiasts should be on the Iconografix mailing list and are invited to write and ask for a catalog, free of charge.

Authors and editors in the field of transportation history are invited to contact the Editorial Department at Iconografix, Inc., PO Box 446, Hudson, WI 54016. We require a minimum of 120 photographs per subject. We prefer subjects narrow in focus, e.g., a specific model, railroad, or racing venue. Photographs must be of high-quality, suited to large format reproduction.

Frank Williams, seen here in his Formula 3 car at the Ring Djursland circuit in Denmark in 1967, was never a great racing driver - but he went on to create the most successful team in Formula One history...

INTRODUCTION

With nine Formula One Constructors' World Championship titles from 1980-1997, Williams has every right to consider itself the most successful team in Formula One. And if you consider the fact that the Williams team made their Formula One debut in 1969 (while their competitors on the all-time record list, Ferrari and McLaren, had their first Formula One Grand Prix in 1950 and 1966 respectively), there is no doubt that Frank Williams and his cars are the biggest success story of modern Grand Prix racing.

But it wasn't always like that. In fact, the story of Frank Williams and his cars is full of both tragedy and triumph. If nothing else, it proves that Frank Williams is a true fighter.

Perhaps part of Frank's fighter instinct comes from his father, who was a RAF pilot during the war. However, Frank's father left their home in the North of England shortly after his son was born in 1942. It was up to Frank's mother, a schoolteacher, and his grandparents to take care of him. He went to boarding school in Dumfries, Scotland, and soon developed a keen interest in motor racing. In 1958 he attended his first race, the British Grand Prix at Silverstone.

As soon as he was old enough for a license, Frank was racing, starting in an Austin at Oulton Park in 1961. It was always a financial fight for young Frank to continue racing. Even though he enjoyed some success in Formula 3, and even made it into a single Formula 2 race - the non-championship "Suomen Grand Prix" in Finland in 1966 - he began to realize that his real talent in motor racing lay in team management and dealing with second-hand racing cars and parts. A prominent "wheeler-dealer" on the British racing scene in the 1960s, Frank became famous for making deals right, left and center, but he also managed to establish his own team, Frank Williams Racing Cars.

Frank Williams Racing Cars entered several drivers in Formula 2 in 1968. Among others entered were Frank's close friend, Piers Courage (heir to the Courage brewery group), and current FIA President Max Mosley. However, Formula One was always Frank Williams' ambition, and in 1969 he realized this. He had used Brabham cars in both Formula 2 and the Tasman series in Australia and New Zealand, but his cunning business brain quickly realized that Brabham was unlikely to sell their latest model to a competitor. So he had to get his 1969 Brabham from an alternative source. Frank discovered that Brabham had sold a 1969 model to a part-time driver in North England who never intended to use it for Grand Prix racing. He bought this car - Frank Williams, 26 years old, was now ready to fight the Big Boys in Formula One like Ferrari, Lotus, McLaren, Tyrrell - and Brabham.

1969 was a great success for Frank Williams Racing Cars. The team's Brabham took Piers Courage to eighth place in the 1970 Drivers' Championship. The following year, again with Courage behind the wheel, Williams ran a car for the Italian De Tomaso factory. But tragedy struck for the first time in the team's brief Formula One career. Courage was killed during the Dutch Grand Prix. Despite his personal loss, Frank Williams fought on, and having missed only one Grand Prix, the team was back on the grid less than a month after the tragedy in Holland.

Not unsurprisingly, De Tomaso lost interest in Formula One. In 1971 and 1972 Williams ran March cars without much success; and the first car designed and built by Frank Williams and his team, financed and named after Italian model car company Politoys, was destroyed by French driver Henri Pescarolo in its debut race, the 1972 British Grand Prix.

A new partnership with Italian sports car manufacturer Iso Rivolta saw Williams cars, at first based on the original Politoys design, take part in the 1973 and 1974 World Championships with a long line of more or less - usually "less" - talented "rent-a-drivers". Money was tighter than ever, and Frank Williams often had to conduct his business from the phone booth outside his backyard factory because the connection inside had been cut off due to unpaid bills. Frank Williams was rapidly gaining a reputation as Formula One's worst "wheeler-dealer" and the sport's eternal loser. His only win came in 1973 when the organizers of the Italian Grand Prix put on a foot race around the Monza circuit. Impressive prize money tempted many of the supposedly top fit drivers to take part, but long distance runner Frank won in dominant fashion - probably because he needed the prize money for his budget!

In 1975 Williams scored a somewhat lucky second place with France's Jacques Laffite behind the wheel in the German Grand Prix. When a new partnership with Austro-Canadian oilman Walter Wolf was announced for 1976, it seemed that the Williams Formula One team was finally on its way.

But things actually went from bad to worse. The 1976 cars, purchased from the defunct Hesketh team, were uncompetitive, and the relationship between Frank Williams and Walter Wolf deteriorated to the point where the oil-millionaire hired a new team manager to replace Williams.

It was back to square one for Frank Williams. Since Wolf had purchased "Frank Williams Racing Cars", Frank had to found a new company, which he named "Williams Grand Prix Engineering". The small team entered a March for Belgium's Patrick Neve in 1977. It was during this season, which saw Neve's seventh place in the American Grand Prix as the team's best result, that Williams finally got his big break. As always, his ear was close to the ground when it came to potential backers. When he heard that some Saudi Arabian businessmen were staying at London's Dorchester Hotel, he painted one of his Formula One cars in the colors of the Saudis, put it on a trailer, towed it up to London and parked it outside the hotel. Legend has it that he waited several days before the Saudis came out of the hotel, saw the car, and shortly afterward decided to support the enthusiastic team owner.

It was the deal Frank Williams had always dreamed. The Arabs were very enthusiastic, and money was obviously not a problem. Some of the executives from the airline Saudia wanted to visit the British Grand Prix at Silverstone. They asked Frank if they could land at the circuit - they had heard that the circuit was once an airfield. When Frank told them that the old runways were not quite long enough, the Arabs just asked how long it would take and how much it would cost to lengthen them. When the team needed extra money, all that was needed was a call to Saudi Arabia, and the money arrived a few days later - probably handed over in a brown envelope at a car park somewhere!

In the beginning, Williams Grand Prix Engineering had just six employees, one of them Patrick Head, a young designer who had left Wolf. Head designed the Williams FW06 for 1978. With Alan Jones behind the wheel and money from Saudi Arabia, Williams never looked back. Several strong races in 1978 and ninth place in the Constructors' Championship were followed by Williams' first Grand Prix win in 1979 - scored by Switzerland's Clay Regazzoni at Silverstone, the very circuit where Frank Williams saw his first motor race 21 years earlier.

In the 1980s, Williams firmly established itself as one of the leading teams in Formula One. The first World Championship titles - for both drivers (Alan Jones) and constructors - were won in 1980. When the Saudi Arabian sponsors left, several Western companies were ready to take over and make sure the financial hardship of the 1970s was a thing of the past. Having run Ford V-8 engines since the debut in 1969, Williams entered a new partnership with Honda in 1983. By now, Formula One's era for normally aspirated engines was coming to an end, and the Japanese V-6 turbo engine went on to become one of the dominant engines of the turbo era.

But, before Williams had won its first World Championship title with Honda, tragedy struck again. Just before the start of the 1986 season, Frank Williams was on his way to the Nice Airport after a test session at the Circuit Paul Ricard, when his car crashed. The accident left fitness freak Frank Williams confined to a wheelchair and almost claimed his life. But once again, Williams showed his amazing fighting spirit. He was back

in the Formula One paddock at the British Grand Prix in July. The team won World Championship titles in both 1986 and 1987, proving just how big and well managed Williams Grand Prix Engineering had become since 1977. . .

Despite winning the Constructors' Championship in 1987, Williams had a controversial season. Frank Williams insisted on letting his drivers, Nelson Piquet and Nigel Mansell, fight for the title without team orders. The end result was that McLaren's Alain Prost won the Drivers' title. Honda was not very impressed by the strong-willed Williams, and - perhaps - also had reservations about the image of a Formula One boss in a wheelchair. The partnership with Williams ended with short notice at the end of 1987. The privately developed, normally aspirated Judd V-8 engines were used as a stop-gap solution in 1988 before Williams entered a new partnership with Renault in 1989. With the French V-10 engines, Williams went on to win several World Championship titles in the 1990s - but again, not without tragedy.

In 1983, Frank Williams had given a young Formula 3 driver by the name of Ayrton Senna da Silva his first test in a Formula One car, but the young Brazilian signed with the Toleman team for his Formula One debut in 1984. Through the 1980s and early 1990s, Ayrton Senna, now driving for McLaren, was often the Williams drivers' toughest opponent. But Frank Williams and Senna always stayed in touch, and a firm friendship was established. Then, in 1994, the "Dream Marriage" between Williams and Senna was finally announced, but the partnership between Frank Williams and the driver he probably admired more than anybody else lasted only a few months. Senna was killed in the 1994 San Marino Grand Prix at Imola. As usual, Frank Williams and his team fought back, winning the Constructors' title in 1994 and then winning both Drivers' and Constructors' titles in 1996 (Damon Hill) and 1997 (Jacques Villeneuve).

By now, the ex wheeler-dealer of the 1970s was a very rich man indeed. In 1998, the Sunday Times estimated Frank Williams' personal fortune to £85 million, giving him a solid 25th place in the paper's list of the top 1000 richest in Britain.

Renault decided to withdraw from Formula One at the end of 1997. The 1998 season, with Renault based but privately developed Mecachrome engines, was not very successful. With a new partnership with BMW not coming off steam until the year 2000, Frank Williams and his team was again facing a crisis.

But as "Fighting Frank" has proved so often, his team is never down for long - it would be very unwise to bet against Williams winning World Championship titles in the new millennium.

1969 was Frank Williams' first season as a Formula One team owner. He entered a Brabham BT26 for his great friend Piers Courage, who took second place in Monaco (photo).

In 1970, Williams ran a car for the Italian De Tomaso factory, but the promising project was struck by tragedy when Piers Courage crashed fatally in the Dutch Grand Prix.

1971 saw Frank Williams enter a March 711 for Henri Pescarolo. The Frenchman, seen here at the Nürburgring during the German Grand Prix, scored four points.

From the very start of its Formula One career, Williams used Ford's Cosworth V-8 engine. Here it is shown in the team's March chassis at the 1971 Spanish Grand Prix.

Williams continued with March chassis in 1972, and Brazil's Carlos Pace, pictured here in the Monaco Grand Prix, scored three points in a promising debut year.

Carlos Pace and Frank Williams before the 1972 Monaco Grand Prix. The Brazilian was one of Frank's first "discoveries" in Formula One, but he left the team after the 1972 season.

1972 saw the first Formula One car designed by Frank Williams' team, the Politoys FX3, debut in the British Grand Prix (photo). It was destroyed in its first race by Henri Pescarolo.

For 1973, Frank Williams entered a new partnership with Italian sports car manufacturer Iso Rivolta. Here, Frank poses with his 1973 car and driver Nanni Galli.

When Nanni Galli suddenly retired from racing, Denmark's Tom Belsø was drafted to the team for the 1973 Swedish Grand Prix, but he didn't start in the race.

New Zealand's Howden Ganley, seen here in the U.S. Grand Prix, was Williams' regular driver in 1973, and he scored a single point in the World Championship.

In 1974, still in partnership with Iso Rivolta, Williams was one of the smallest teams in Formula One, and team owner Frank Williams (left) was also in charge of the pit board.

As a driver, Frank Williams never made it into Formula One, but at least he later had the chance to sit in one of his cars - here at the 1974 Spanish Grand Prix.

Tom Belsø was one of several drivers entered by Williams in 1974. The Dane left the team after he failed to qualify for the British Grand Prix at Brands Hatch (photo).

France's Jacques Laffite, seen here retiring from the Dutch Grand Prix, was Williams' regular driver in 1975, when the team actually entered a total of 10 different drivers!

Ian Scheckter drove a couple of races for Williams in 1975 without much success. Here the South African crashes out of the Swedish Grand Prix due to a burst tire.

Frank Williams quickly established a reputation as one of Formula One's great talent spotters. In late 1975 he gave Gunnar Nillson his first test in Formula One at Goodwood.

In 1976, Frank Williams teamed up with Austro-Canadian oilman Walter Wolf, and bought the Hesketh team's 1975 cars for Jacky Ickx (photo) and other drivers.

France's Michel Leclere, here in the Swedish Grand Prix, was one of several drivers who tried the unsuccessful 1976 car, which was based on the 1975 Hesketh.

Having split with Walter Wolf, Frank Williams created "Williams Grand Prix Engineering" for 1977, and entered Belgian's Patrick Neve in a March (here in Swedish Grand Prix).

As a "new" team, Williams had only rather primitive paddock facilities in 1977. Here, mechanics work on the team's March at the British Grand Prix at Silverstone.

The FW06 from 1978 was the first Formula One car designed by Williams Grand Prix Engineering's Technical Director Patrick Head. Here is Alan Jones in the U.S. Grand Prix West.

The 1978 Williams FW06, here in the pits at Holland's Zandvoort circuit, was a fairly simple and robust car, which scored 11 points with Alan Jones behind the wheel.

Alan Jones joined Williams for 1978, and the tough Australian was one of the leading lights in Williams' transformation from "also-ran" to "top-team" (here in 1978 Swedish Grand Prix).

Swiss veteran Clay Regazzoni joined Williams for 1979 and scored the team's first Grand Prix win at Silverstone, Great Britain. Here "Regga" is seen in the FW07 at Zandvoort, Holland.

Alan Jones, here leading Gilles Villeneuve's Ferrari in the Dutch Grand Prix, was the fastest driver of 1979, but technical problems meant he only finished third in the World Championship.

The FW07 from 1979 was Patrick Head's first "wing car", and it secured second place for Williams behind Ferrari in the Constructors' World Championship.

In 1980, Alan Jones won the Drivers' World Championship. With teammate Carlos Reutemann, he made sure that Williams took the first of many Constructors' titles.

By 1980, Williams had developed into a well-organized top team. Here, mechanics change wheels on Alan Jones' Williams FW07B during practice for the British Grand Prix.

Alan Jones on his way to third place in the 1980 German Grand Prix. On his way to the World Championship, the Australian took five Grand Prix wins.

Technical Director Patrick Head (left) and Team Owner Frank Williams in the pits during the 1980 German Grand Prix. The talented duo made Williams a top team.

The controversial 1981 season started with the non-championship South African Grand Prix at Kyalami. Alan Jones retired from the race with a damaged skirt.

In 1981, Carlos Reutemann (pictured in the U.S. West Grand Prix) and teammate Alan Jones took Williams to another Constructors' Championship. The Drivers' Title went to Brabham's Nelson Piquet.

Despite other top teams running turbo engines, Williams stayed with the normally aspirated Ford Cosworth V-8 for 1982, and Keke Rosberg (pictured in Monaco) won the championship in the reliable FW08.

Keke Rosberg fought a heroic fight against the more powerful turbo cars in 1982 - especially at the faster circuits like Germany's Hockenheim (photo).

One of Williams' answers to other teams' turbo engines was this six-wheeler. It tested in 1981-1982, but never raced, and for 1983 new rules meant that only four wheels were allowed.

By 1983, the turbo cars were dominant, but reigning World Champion Keke Rosberg still won Brands Hatch's non-championship Race of Champions in his normally aspirated Williams.

Keke Rosberg often performed miracles with the under-powered, normally aspirated FW08C in 1983. Here, the "Flying Finn" is seen in the Detroit Grand Prix.

For the European Grand Prix in 1983, Williams entered a third car for Britain's Jonathan Palmer. It was the first time, and so far the only time Williams had three cars in a Grand Prix.

For the 1983 end-of-season South African Grand Prix, Williams finally got a turbo engine. Patrick Head and Keke Rosberg admire the new Honda V-6 at Kyalami.

1984 saw Keke Rosberg score Williams' first turbo win in the U.S. Dallas Grand Prix in July, but the season was also frustrated by reliability problems.

Jacques Laffite, who had driven for Williams in the difficult mid-1970s, returned to the team in 1983-1984. Here the popular Frenchman is spinning at Zandvoort in 1984.

The Williams FW09 and the "B" version introduced at mid-season in 1984 had lots of power from the Honda V-6 turbo engine - and, to begin with, lots of problems...

In 1984 Williams moved into a new purpose-built HQ in Didcot. The towers in the background are from the team's neighbor, Didcot Power Station.

The Williams FW10 of 1985 was a far more elegant design than the 1984 FW09. Keke Rosberg, here in the Brazilian Grand Prix, took third place in the championship.

Williams was dominant in the final races of the 1985 World Championship, winning the last three races. This is Keke Rosberg in the European Grand Prix at Brands Hatch.

Nelson Piquet joined Williams for 1986. Here, the Brazilian is seen during pre-season testing at Estoril with Frank Williams (right) and designer Frank Dernie (left).

Following his car accident in early 1986, Frank Williams made a welcome return to Formula One at the British Grand Prix. To the left Nigel Mansell, right Nelson Piquet.

Nelson Piquet leading Nigel Mansell during the 1986 German Grand Prix. The Williams drivers were often in a class of their own, but fought so hard that Alain Prost (McLaren) won the Drivers' Championship.

Don't be fooled. The relationship between Williams drivers Nigel Mansell (left) and Nelson Piquet (here at Hungaroring) was not very good during the 1986 season.

Nelson Piquet leaves the pits at Mexico's Autodromo Hermanos Rodriguez in October 1986. The Brazilian finished fourth in the race.

Nelson Piquet won the 1987 World Championship for Williams - and then left the team to go to Lotus. Here the Brazilian poses for photographers before his home Grand Prix in Rio de Janeiro.

Nigel Mansell was - again - desperately unlucky in 1987. Here he heads for the pits with a damaged rear tire in the Brazilian Grand Prix in Rio de Janeiro.

The FW11B of 1987, here in the French Grand Prix with Mansell behind the wheel, took Williams to another Constructors' Championship, but it was also the last Honda powered Williams.

Following Honda's withdrawal, Williams was "between partners" in 1988. The team had to use the uncompetitive, normally aspirated Judd V-8 engine for the FW12 (here in Monaco Grand Prix with Mansell behind the wheel).

Despite the lack of horsepower - compared to the turbocharged opposition - an inspired Nigel Mansell took the normally aspirated Williams FW12 to second place in the 1988 British Grand Prix.

Technical Director Patrick Head telling Nigel Mansell that the Williams FW12 is 300 horsepower down on the turbocharged opposition. Not quite, but Williams was far behind their more powerful rivals in 1987.

In June 1988, Williams signed a new, three-year engine contract with Renault. From left to right, Renault's Technical Manager Bernard Dudot, Williams' Technical Director Patrick Head, Renault Sport's General Manager Bernard Casin and Frank Williams celebrate the new deal.

For most of the 1989 season, Williams entered a "C" version of the FW12. Here, Riccardo Patrese tests the first Renault powered Williams at Jerez in Spain in early 1989.

Thierry Boutsen, seen here during the San Marino Grand Prix in Imola, joined Williams for 1989 and scored the team's first Grand Prix win with Renault power in Canada.

The Williams FW12C, here driven by Patrese in the Monaco Grand Prix, took Williams to second place in the 1988 Constructors' World Championship.

Riccardo Patrese, here in practice for the season-opener U.S. Grand Prix in Phoenix, finished seventh in the 1990 World Championship with the Williams FW13B.

For Thierry Boutsen, 1990 was his second and last season with Williams. The Belgian, here in the U.S. Grand Prix in Phoenix, won one race in the 1990 FW13B.

Riccardo Patrese celebrates his win in the 1990 San Marino Grand Prix in Imola. He is driving the "B" version of the Williams FW13, which was used all season.

For most of the 1991 season, this was the view for Williams' opposition. The FW14 was the best chassis, but the year was hampered by early-season gearbox problems.

70

Nigel Mansell (front) and Riccardo Patrese finished second and third in the 1991 World Championship and made sure Williams was runner-up behind McLaren in the Constructors' Championship.

Riccardo Patrese (left) and Nigel Mansell is the most successful Williams driver line-up. In 1991 and 1992 they scored eight one-two wins for the team.

Nigel Mansell began his 1992 championship campaign with an unparalleled five wins in a row. Here he celebrates the historic fifth win - in the San Marino Grand Prix - with teammate Riccardo Patrese.

The view Williams' opposition did not enjoy in 1992 - watching Williams from behind. The FW14B was in a class of its own in what was one of Grand Prix racing's most "high-tech" year ever.

Riccardo Patrese, here in the Italian Grand Prix, was a solid back up for Nigel Mansell in 1992, and the experienced Italian finished second in the World Championship.

Williams had an all-new line-up for 1993 with Alain Prost (left) coming back from retirement and the team's test driver, Damon Hill, being promoted to the race team.

Damon Hill had a difficult start to his first full Formula One season in 1993. Here he has spun off in the San Marino Grand Prix at Imola.

As the 1993 season progressed, Damon Hill (left) moved closer and closer to team mate Alain Prost, and the Englishman took a fine third place in the World Championship.

Alain Prost, in his final year as a Formula One driver, won the 1993 World Championship. One of his few mistakes came in practice for the Portuguese Grand Prix (picture).

In 1994, more than 10 years after Frank Williams gave Ayrton Senna a Formula One test, he finally signed the great Brazilian.

The partnership between Formula One's best team, Williams, and the greatest driver, Ayrton Senna, was short-lived. The Brazilian was killed in a tragic accident during the San Marino Grand Prix at Imola.

After Senna's death, Damon Hill (left) was promoted to team leader, and the young test driver, David Coulthard, moved onto the race team.

Nigel Mansell, seen here making a pit stop in the European Grand Prix, returned to Williams for a few races in 1994, winning the Australian Grand Prix in Adeaide.

In 1995, Williams entered David Coulthard (front) and Damon Hill in the FW17. The team's plans were announced at a pre-season conference at Portugal's Estoril circuit (picture).

Damon Hill took the lead at the start of the 1995 Monaco Grand Prix. But behind him, teammate David Coulthard was pushed into a frightening flight. No one was injured in the crash, but the race was red-flagged.

Damon Hill fought long and hard with Michael Schumacher (Benetton-Renault) for the 1995 title, but he eventually lost out to the German. Here Hill spins during the wet Belgian Grand Prix.

Team debriefing in the Williams motor home during 1995. From left to right, David Coulthard, Chief Designer Adrian Reynard, Coulthard's race engineer Jock Clear, Hill's race engineer David Brown and Damon Hill.

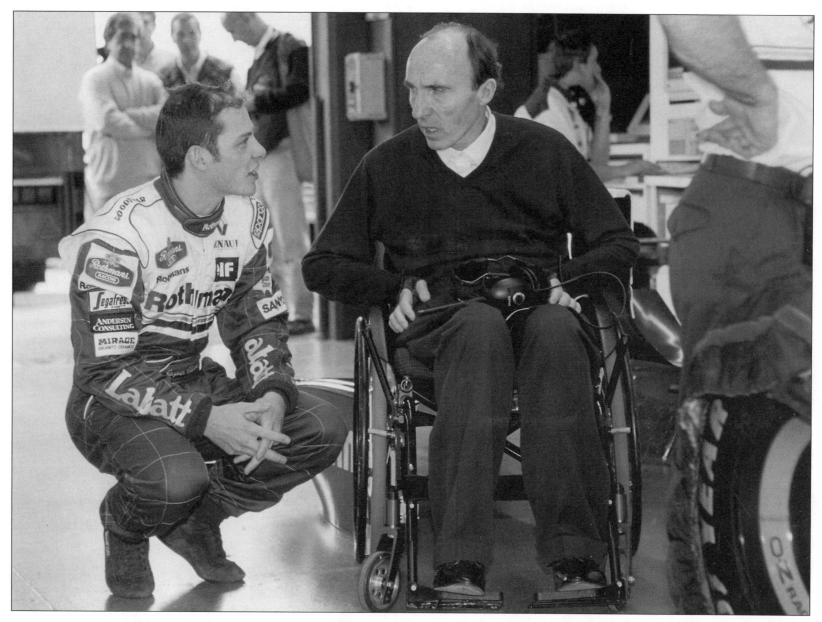

In 1995, Frank Williams invited IndyCar Champion Jacques Villeneuve to a series of tests, and the young Canadian was signed for 1996. The photo shows Villeneuve and Williams during a test at Monza in September.

Jacques Villeneuve quickly adapted to Formula One. Seen here in the Argentinian Grand Prix in Buenos Aires, the Canadian fought teammate Damon Hill for the 1996 World Champion.

Williams has always been famous for its efficient pit work. Here, mechanics service Damon Hill on his way to second place in the 1996 Hungarian Grand Prix.

With arch rival Michael Schumacher in an uncompetitive Ferrari, the 1996 World Champion was a fight between Williams teammates Damon Hill and Jacques Villeneuve. Hill (pictured) won.

By 1996, Williams Grand Prix Engineering was employing close to 250 people, and the Didcot HQ was rapidly becoming too small. A new factory in Grove, outside Oxford, was opened by Her Royal Highness Princess Anne in October 1996.

Damon Hill left Williams after the 1996 season, and Jacques Villeneuve was promoted to team leader for 1997. The Canadian's Championship campaign got off to a bad start when he spun out of the opening race, the Australian Grand Prix.

For 1997, Bridgestone entered Formula One, but Williams stayed loyal to Goodyear. The "Tyre War" saw Villeneuve win the Spanish Grand Prix on very blistered tires (photo).

1997 was Renault's final year in Formula One. Williams said "good-bye" to its engine partner since 1989 with the Drivers' Championship to Villeneuve (right) and another Constructors' Championship.

Heinz-Harald Frentzen joined Williams for 1997, but even though the German – seen here in the Canadian Grand Prix - won at Imola, he was rarely a match for Villeneuve.

1998 saw Williams run the Renault-based but privately developed Mecachrome engines. Heinz-Harald Frentzen, seen here during the Brazilian Grand Prix, had an uncompetitive season.

Jacques Villeneuve, seen here in the Canadian Grand Prix, fought hard with the Williams FW20 during 1998. When a new version with extended wheelbase was introduced at mid-season, the Canadian made Williams competitive once again.

Heinz-Harald Frentzen was a disappointment in 1998, and his contract was not renewed. With Villeneuve also leaving the team, Williams had to face 1999 with a totally new line-up.

The man behind Williams' success. Patrick Head, Technical Director since Williams Grand Prix Engineering was founded, poses with the FW19 at the Didcot factory.

Drivers who scored World Championship points with Williams.

Piers Courage (GB),
born May 27, 1942 (killed in Dutch
Grand Prix 1970)
Drove for Williams 1969-1970

Henri Pescarolo (F),
born September 25, 1942
Drove for Williams 1971-1973

Carlos Pace (BR), born October 6,
1944 (killed in airplane accident 1977)
Drove for Williams 1972

Gijs van Lennep (NL),
born March 16, 1942
Drove for Williams 1973-1974

Howden Ganley (NZ),
born December 24, 1941
Drove for Williams 1973

Arturo Merzario (I),
born March 11, 1943
Drove for Williams 1974-1976

Jacques Laffite (F),
born November 21, 1943
Drove for Williams 1974-1975 and
1983-1984

Alan Jones (AUS),
born November 2, 1946
Drove for Williams 1978-1981

Clay Regazzoni (CH),
born September 5, 1939
Drove for Williams 1979

Carlos Reutemann (RA),
born April 12, 1942
Drove for Williams 1980-1982

Keke Rosberg (SF),
born December 6, 1948
Drove for Williams 1982-1985

Derek Daly (IRL), born March 11, 1953
Drove for Williams 1982

Nigel Mansell (GB),
born August 8, 1953
Drove for Williams 1985-1988,
1991-1992 and 1994

Nelson Piquet (BR),
born August 17, 1952
Drove for Williams 1986-1987

Riccardo Patrese (I),
born April 17, 1954
Drove for Williams 1987-1992

Thierry Boutsen (B),
born July 13, 1957
Drove for Williams 1989-1990

Alain Prost (F),
born February 24, 1955
Drove for Williams 1993

Damon Hill (GB),
born September 17, 1960
Drove for Williams 1993-1996

David Coulthard (GB),
born March 27, 1971
Drove for Williams 1994-1995

Jacques Villeneuve (CDN),
born April 9, 1971
Drove for Williams 1996-1998

Heinz-Harald Frentzen (D),
born May 18, 1967
Drove for Williams 1997-1998

Williams in Formula One:

1969:
Company: Frank Williams Racing Cars
Entrant: Frank Williams Racing Cars
No. of Grand Prix entered: 10 of 11
Car: Brabham BT26 – Engine: Ford V-8
Designer: Ron Tauranac (Brabham)
Driver(s): Piers Courage (GB)
World Championship points: Courage: 16 (8th.)
Position in Constructors' World Champion: - (points scored with Brabham chassis)
Notes: Frank Williams' first year as a Formula One entrant. During 1969, the team also entered two non-championship Formula One races with Courage.

1970:
Company: Frank Williams Racing Cars
Entrant: Frank Williams Racing Cars
No. of Grand Prix entered: 11 of 13
Car: De Tomaso 505 – Engine: Ford V-8
Designer: Giampaolo Dall'Ara (De Tomaso)
Driver(s): Piers Courage (GB), Brian Redman (GB), Tim Schenken (AUS)
World Championship points: -
Position in Constructors' World Champion: -
Notes: Piers Courage killed at Dutch Grand Prix in June. During 1970, the team also entered two non-championship Formula One races with Courage and Schenken.

1971:
Company: Frank Williams Racing Cars
Entrant: Frank Williams Racing Cars
No. of Grand Prix entered: 11 of 11
Car: March 701 and 711 – Engine: Ford V-8
Designer: Robin Herd (March)
Driver(s): Henri Pescarolo (F), Jean Max (F)
World Championship points: Pescarolo: 4 (16th.)
Position in Constructors' World Champion: - (points scored with March chassis)
Notes: First time Williams enters two cars in Grand Prix (France). During 1971, the team also entered six non-championship Formula One races with drivers Ronnie Peterson, Ray Allen, Derek Bell, Cyd Williams, Tony Trimmer as well as Pescarolo.

1972:
Company: Frank Williams Racing Cars
Entrant: Team Williams Motul
No. of Grand Prix entered: 12 of 12
Car: March 711 & 721; Politoys FX3 – Engine: Ford V-8
Designer: Robin Herd (March), Len Bailey (Politoys)
Driver(s): Henri Pescarolo (F), Carlos Pace (BR)
World Championship points: Pace: 3 (18th.)
Position in Constructors' World Champion: - (points scored with March chassis)
Notes: First genuine Williams car, called Politoys, destroyed in debut race. During 1972, the team also entered five non-championship Formula One races with drivers Reine Wisell (non-starter in Brazilian Grand Prix in a Surtees !) and Chris Amon as well as Pescarolo and Pace.

1973:
Company: Frank Williams Racing Cars
Entrant: Frank Williams Racing Cars
No. of Grand Prix entered: 15 of 15
Car: Iso-Williams FX3B and Iso-Williams IR – Engine: Ford V-8
Designer: Len Bailey (FX3B) and John Clarke (IR)
Driver(s): Howden Ganley (NZ), Nanni Galli (I), Jackie Pretorius (ZA), Tom Belsø (DK), Henri Pescarolo (F), Graham McRae (NZ), Gijs van Lennep (NL), Tim Schenken (AUS), Jacky Ickx (B).
World Championship points: van Lennep: 1 (19th.) Ganley: 1 (19th.)
Position in Constructors' World Champion: 10th. - 2 points
Notes: FX-cars, used for first three Grand Prix, based on 1972 Politoys. During 1973, the team also entered two non-championship Formula One races with Tony Trimmer and Ganley.

1974:
Company: Frank Williams Racing Cars
Entrant: Frank Williams Racing Cars
No. of Grand Prix entered: 15 of 15
Car: Iso-Williams FW – Engine: Ford V-8
Designer: John Clarke
Driver(s): Arturo Merzario (I), Tom Belsø (DK), Gijs van Lennep (NL), Richard Robarts (GB), Jean-Pierre Jabouille (F), Jacques Laffite (F)
World Championship points: Merzario: 4 (17th.)
Position in Constructors' World Champion: 10th. - 4 points
Notes: During 1974, the team also entered one non-championship Formula One race with Merzario.

1975:
Company: Frank Williams Racing Cars
Entrant: Frank Williams Racing Cars
No. of Grand Prix entered: 14 of 14
Car: Williams FW03 and FW04 – Engine: Ford V-8
Designer: John Clarke (FW03) and Ray Stokoe (FW04)
Driver(s): Arturo Merzario (I), Jacques Laffite (I), Tony Brise (GB), Damien Magee (GB), Ian Scheckter (ZA), Francois Migault (F), Ian Ashley (GB), Jo Vonlanthen (CH), Renzo Zorzi (I), Lella Lombardi (I).
World Championship points: Laffite: 6 (12th.)
Position in Constructors' World Champion: 9th. with 6 points
Notes: A record year: Williams entered 10 different drivers for the 14 Grand Prix ! During 1975, the team also entered two non-championship Formula One races with Maurizio Flammini as well as Merzario and Vonlanthen.

1976:
Company: Frank Williams Racing Cars
Entrant: Frank Williams Racing Cars; Walter Wolf Racing, Mapfre-Williams
No. of Grand Prix entered: 16 of 16
Car: Wolf-Williams FW04 and FW05 – Engine: Ford V-8
Designer: Ray Stokoe (FW04), Harvey Postlethwaite (FW05)
Driver(s): Jacky Ickx (B), Renzo Zorzi (I), Michel Leclere (F), Emilio Zapico (E), Arturo Merzario (I), Chris Amon (NZ), Warwick Brown (AUS), Hans Binder (A).
World Championship points: -
Position in Constructors' World Champion: -
Notes: Williams enters cooperation with Austro-Canadian oil man Walter Wolf. Old FW04 only used for opening race in Brazil and in Spain for privateer Zapico (entered under the "Mapfre-Williams" banner). During 1976, the team also entered two non-championship Formula One races with Mario Andretti and Ickx. FW05 in reality the 1975 cars bought from Hesketh team. Name of entrant changed from "Frank Williams Racing Cars" to "Walter Wolf Racing" before Spanish Grand Prix. Cars remain "Wolf-Williams". Confused ? So was Frank Williams, who left the team.

1977:
Company: Williams Grand Prix Engineering
Entrant: Williams Grand Prix Engineering
No. of Grand Prix entered: 11 of 17
Car: March 761 – Engine: Ford V-8
Designer: Robin Herd (March) (March modified by Patrick Head)
Driver(s): Patrick Neve (B)
World Championship points: -
Position in Constructors' World Champion: -
Notes: As "Frank Williams Racing Cars" was taken over by Walter Wolf, Frank Williams founded "Williams Grand Prix Engineering", which made its debut in the Spanish Grand Prix with an old March chassis.

1978:
Company: Williams Grand Prix Engineering
Entrant: Williams Grand Prix Engineering
No. of Grand Prix entered: 16 of 16
Car: Williams FW06 – Engine: Ford V-8
Designer: Patrick Head
Driver(s): Alan Jones (AUS)
World Championship points: Jones: 11 (11th.)
Position in Constructors' World Champion: 9th. with 11 points

Notes: Williams attracts Saudi Arabian sponsors, and Patrick Head designs his first F1 car, the FW06.

1979:
Company: Williams Grand Prix Engineering
Entrant: Albilad-Saudia Racing Team
No. of Grand Prix entered: 15 of 15
Car: Williams FW07 – Engine: Ford V-8
Designer: Patrick Head
Driver(s): Alan Jones (AUS), Clay Regazzoni (CH)
World Championship points: Jones: 40 (3rd.) Regazzoni 29 (5th.)
Position in Constructors' World Champion: 2nd. with 75 points
Notes: Regazzoni takes Williams' first Grand Prix win in British Grand Prix.

1980:
Company: Williams Grand Prix Engineering
Entrant: Albilad-Williams Racing Team
No. of Grand Prix entered: 14 of 14
Car: Williams FW07 and 07B – Engine: Ford V-8
Designer: Patrick Head
Driver(s): Alan Jones (AUS), Carlos Reutemann (RA)
World Championship points: Jones: 67 (1st.) Reutemann: 42 (3rd.)
Position in Constructors' World Champion: FIRST with 120 points
Notes: "B" version of FW07 introduced at opening race. First Constructors' and Drivers' World Championship titles to Williams.

1981:
Company: Williams Grand Prix Engineering
Entrant: Albilad-Williams Racing Team
No. of Grand Prix entered: 15 of 15
Car: Williams FW07C – Engine: Ford V-8
Designer: Patrick Head
Driver(s): Alan Jones (AUS), Carlos Reutemann (RA)
World Championship points: Reutemann: 49 (2nd.) Jones: 46 (3rd.)
Position in Constructors' World Champion: FIRST with 95 points
Notes: "C" version of FW07 used all year. FW07D, a six-wheeler with four rear-wheels, is tested towards the end of the year, but never raced. Developments continued until a ban on six-wheelers in Formula One was introduced for 1983. In February 1981, Williams took part in the non-championship South African Grand Prix, which was won by Reutemann.

1982:
Company: Williams Grand Prix Engineering
Entrant: TAG Williams Team
No. of Grand Prix entered: 15 of 16
Car: Williams FW07C and FW08 – Engine: Ford V-8

Designer: Patrick Head
Driver(s): Keke Rosberg (SF), Carlos Reutemann (RA), Mario Andretti (USA), Derek Daly (IRL)
World Championship points: Rosberg: 44 (1st.) Daly: 8 (13th.) Reutemann: 6 (15th.).
Position in Constructors' World Champion: 4th. with 58 points
Notes: New FW08 introduced for Belgian Grand Prix in May. Williams boycotted San Marino Grand Prix along with other British teams. Reutemann retires after second race and is replaced by Andretti in Long Beach Grand Prix in April and then Daly for rest if season.

1983:
Company: Williams Grand Prix Engineering
Entrant: TAG Williams Team
No. of Grand Prix entered: 15 of 15
Car: Williams FW08C and 09 – Engine: Ford V-8 (FW08C) and Honda V-6 Turbo (FW09)
Designer: Patrick Head
Driver(s): Keke Rosberg (SF), Jacques Laffite (F), Jonathan Palmer (GB)
World Championship points: Rosberg: 27 (5th.) Laffite: 11 (11th.)
Position in Constructors' World Champion: 4th. with 38 points
Notes: FW08C used all year except for final race in South Africa, when FW09 with Honda V-6 Turbo engine makes its debut - this is the first non-Ford powered Williams. Palmer entered as third driver for European Grand Prix in September. This is first and only time Williams enters three cars in a Grand Prix. Formula 3 driver Ayrton Senna tests for team. Rosberg wins non-championship Race of Champions on Brands Hatch.

1984:
Company: Williams Grand Prix Engineering
Entrant: Williams Grand Prix Engineering
No. of Grand Prix entered: 16 of 16
Car: Williams FW09 and 09B – Engine: Honda V-6 Turbo
Designer: Patrick Head
Driver(s): Keke Rosberg (SF), Jacques Laffite (F)
World Championship points: Rosberg: 20,5 (8th.) Laffite: 5 (14th.)
Position in Constructors' World Champion: 6th. with 25.5 points
Notes: "B" version of FW09 introduced at mid-season. Rosberg scores Williams' and Honda's first turbo-win in Dallas Grand Prix in July. Williams Grand Prix Engineering moves into new custom-built H.Q. in Didcot.

1985:
Company: Williams Grand Prix Engineering
Entrant: Canon Williams Honda Team

No. of Grand Prix entered: 16 of 16
Car: Williams FW10 – Engine: Honda V-6 Turbo
Designer: Patrick Head
Driver(s): Keke Rosberg (SF), Nigel Mansell (GB)
World Championship points: Rosberg: 40 (3rd.) Mansell: 31 (6th.)
Position in Constructors' World Champion: 3rd. with 71 points
Notes: Williams wins final three Grand Prix of season.

1986:
Company: Williams Grand Prix Engineering
Entrant: Canon Williams Honda Team
No. of Grand Prix entered: 16 of 16
Car: Williams FW11 – Engine: Honda V-6 Turbo
Designer: Patrick Head
Driver(s): Nigel Mansell (GB), Nelson Piquet (BR)
World Championship points: Mansell: 70 (2nd.) Piquet: 69 (3rd.)
Position in Constructors' World Champion: FIRST with 141 points
Notes: Frank Williams is seriously injured in road accident before start of season. Mansell loses Drivers' Championship to Alain Prost (McLaren-TAG) when rear tyre explodes with 19 laps to go in final race.

1987:
Company: Williams Grand Prix Engineering
Entrant: Canon Williams Honda
No. of Grand Prix entered: 16 of 16
Car: Williams FW11B – Engine: Honda V-6 Turbo
Designer: Patrick Head
Driver(s): Nigel Mansell (GB), Nelson Piquet (BR), Riccardo Patrese (I)
World Championship points: Piquet: 73 (1st.) Mansell: 61 (2nd.)
Position in Constructors' World Champion: FIRST with 137 points
Notes: Mansell loses title chances with practice crash in Japanese Grand Prix. The injured Englishman is replaced by Patrese in final race.

1988:
Company: Williams Grand Prix Engineering
Entrant: Canon Williams Team
No. of Grand Prix entered: 16 of 16
Car: Williams FW12 – Engine: Judd V-8
Designer: Patrick Head
Driver(s): Nigel Mansell (GB), Riccardo Partrese (I), Martin Brundle (GB), Jean-Louis Schlesser (F)
World Championship points: Mansell: 12 (9th.) Patrese: 8 (11th.)
Position in Constructors' World Champion: 7th. with 20 points

Notes: Association with Honda ends and Williams is forced to use the uncompetetive Judd V-8 engine. Mansell misses two Grand Prix due to a bout of chicken-pox, and is replaced by Brundle (Belgium) and Schlesser (Italy).

1989:
Company: Williams Grand Prix Engineering
Entrant: Canon Williams Team
No. of Grand Prix entered: 16 of 16
Car: Williams FW12C and FW13 – Engine: Renault V-10
Designer: Patrick Head
Driver(s): Thierry Boutsen (B), Riccardo Patrese (I)
World Championship points: Patrese: 40 (3rd.) Boutsen: 37 (5th.)
Position in Constructors' World Champion: 2nd. with 77 points
Notes: Williams enters new partnership with Renault. FW12C used for most of the season; FW13 introduced for Portugese Grand Prix in September. Boutsen scores Williams first Renault-powered Grand Prix win in Canada.

1990:
Company: Williams Grand Prix Engineering
Entrant: Canon Williams Team
No. of Grand Prix entered: 16 of 16
Car: Williams FW13B – Engine: Renault V-10
Designer: Patrick Head
Driver(s): Thierry Boutsen (B), Riccardo Patrese (I)
World Championship points: Boutsen: 34 (6th.) Patrese: 23 (7th.)
Position in Constructors' World Champion: 4th. with 57 points
Notes: "B" version of FW13 used all year. Patrese and Boutsen score one win each. Aerodynamicist Adrian Newey joins team

1991:
Company: Williams Grand Prix Engineering
Entrant: Canon Williams Team
No. of Grand Prix entered: 16 of 16
Car: Williams FW14 – Engine: Renault V-10
Designer: Patrick Head, Adrian Newey
Driver(s): Nigel Mansell (GB), Riccardo Patrese (I)
World Championship points: Mansell: 72 (2nd.) Patrese: 53 (3rd.)
Position in Constructors' World Champion: 2nd. with 125 points
Notes: The Williams FW14 was probably the best chassis of Formula One 1991, but the season was hampered by the early-season sorting out of new electro-hydraulic gearbox.

1992:
Company: Williams Grand Prix Engineering
Entrant: Canon Williams Team

No. of Grand Prix entered: 16 of 16
Car: Williams FW14B – Engine: Renault V-10
Designer: Patrick Head, Adrian Newey
Driver(s): Nigel Mansell (GB), Riccardo Patrese (I)
World Championship points: Mansell: 108 (1st.) Patrese: 56 (2nd.)
Position in Constructors' World Champion: FIRST with 164 points
Notes: The high-tech FW14B, probably the most advanced Formula One car ever built, is in a class of its own in this record-breaking season for Williams.

1993:
Company: Williams Grand Prix Engineering
Entrant: Canon Williams
No. of Grand Prix entered: 16 of 16
Car: Williams FW15C – Engine: Renault V-10
Designer: Patrick Head, Adrian Newey
Driver(s): Alain Prost (F), Damon Hill (GB)
World Championship points: Prost: 99 (1st.) Hill: 69 (3rd.)
Position in Constructors' World Champion: FIRST with 168 points
Notes: As FW14B was so successful in 1992, its successor, FW15 which was ready in august 1992, never raced. FW15B was the test car for the winter 1992-93, and the FW15C was used in all 1993 races.

1994:
Company: Williams Grand Prix Engineering
Entrant: Rothmans Williams Renault
No. of Grand Prix entered: 16 of 16
Car: Williams FW16 and FW16B – Engine: Renault V-10
Designer: Patrick Head, Adrian Newey
Driver(s): Damon Hill (GB), Ayrton Senna (BR), David Coulthard (GB), Nigel Mansell (GB).
World Championship points: Hill: 91 (2nd.) Coulthard: 14 (8th.) Mansell: 13 (9th.)
Position in Constructors' World Champion: FIRST with 118 points
Notes: Senna joins team, but is killed in San Marino Grand Prix. He is replaced by Coulthard and later Mansell. 16B, with improved aerodynamics, introduced for German Grand Prix.

1995:
Company: Williams Grand Prix Engineering
Entrant: Rothmans Williams Renault
No. of Grand Prix entered: 17 of 17
Car: Williams FW17 and FW17B – Engine: Renault V-10
Designer: Patrick Head, Adrian Newey
Driver(s): Damon Hill (GB), David Coulthard (GB)
World Championship points: Hill: 69 (2nd.) Coulthard: 49 (3rd.)
Position in Constructors' World Champion: 2nd. with 112

points
Notes: FW17B with revised rear-end introduced for European Grand Prix in early October

1996:
Company: Williams Grand Prix Engineering
Entrant: Rothmans Williams Renault
No. of Grand Prix entered: 16 of 16
Car: Williams FW18 – Engine: Renault V-10
Designer: Patrick Head, Adrian Newey
Driver(s): Damon Hill (GB), Jacques Villeneuve (CDN).
World Championship points: Hill: 97 (1st.) Villeneuve: 78 (2nd.)
Position in Constructors' World Champion: FIRST with 175 points
Notes: Team moves into new H.Q. in Grove. Williams wins 12 of 16 races, and championship become "internal affairs" with Hill beating newcomer Villeneuve.

1997:
Company: Williams Grand Prix Engineering
Entrant: Rothmans Williams Renault
No. of Grand Prix entered: 17 of 17
Car: Williams FW19 – Engine: Renault V-10
Designer: Patrick Head
Driver(s): Jacques Villeneuve (CDN), Heinz-Harald Frentzen (D)
World Championship points: Villeneuve: 81 (1st.) Frentzen: 42 (2nd.)
Position in Constructors' World Champion: FIRST with 123 points
Notes: Newey leaves team at mid-season. Renault withdraws from Formula One at end of season, and Williams announce new partnership with BMW from year 2000. The Renault based Mecachrome V-10 to be used in 1998-99.

1998:
Company: Williams Grand Prix Engineering
Entrant: Windfield Williams
No. of Grand Prix entered: 16 of 16
Car: Williams FW20 – Engine: Mecachrome V-10
Designer: Patrick Head
Driver(s): Jacques Villeneuve (CDN), Heinz-Harald Frentzen (D)
World Championship points: Villeneuve: 21 (5th.) Frentzen: 17 (7th.)
Position in Constructors' World Champion: 3rd with 38 points
Notes: Williams 30th. year as a Formula One entrant. The Mecachrome V-10 cannot live up to its Renault predecessor.
Notes: Frank Williams receives a knighthood on the New Year's Honour List

More Titles from Iconografix:

*This product is sold under license from Mack Trucks, Inc. Mack is a registered Trademark of Mack Trucks, Inc. All rights reserved.

All Iconografix books are available from direct mail specialty book dealers and bookstores worldwide, or can be ordered from the publisher. For book trade and distribution information or to add your name to our mailing list contact

Iconografix
PO Box 446
Hudson, Wisconsin, 54016

Telephone: (715) 381-9755
(800) 289-3504 (USA)
Fax: (715) 381-9756

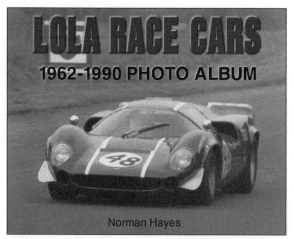
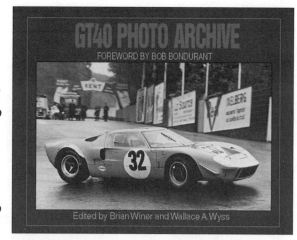
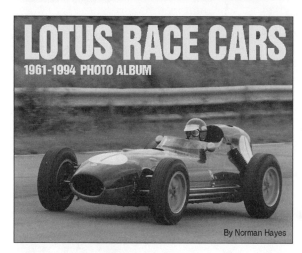
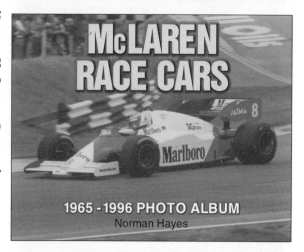

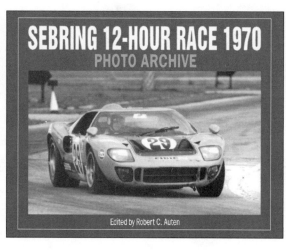